Why Do We Have Creeds?

Basics of the Faith

Am I Called?
How Do We Glorify God?
How Our Children Come to Faith
Is Jesus in the Old Testament?
What Are Election and Predestination?
What Are Spiritual Gifts?
What Happens after Death?
What Is a Reformed Church?
What Is a True Calvinist?
What Is Biblical Preaching?
What Is Church Government?
What Is Discipleship?
What Is Evangelism?
What Is Faith?
What Is Grace?
What Is Hell?
What Is Justification by Faith Alone?
What Is Man?
What Is Mercy Ministry?
What Is Perseverance of the Saints?
What Is Providence?
What Is Regeneration?
What Is Resurrection?
What Is Spiritual Warfare?
What Is the Atonement?
What Is the Bible?
What Is the Christian Worldview?
What Is the Doctrine of Adoption?
What Is the Incarnation?
What Is the Lord's Supper?
What Is the Trinity?
What Is True Conversion?
What Is Vocation?
What Is Worship Music?
Why Believe in God?
Why Do We Baptize Infants?
Why Do We Have Creeds?
Why Do We Pray?
Why God Gave Us a Book

Sean Michael Lucas, Series Editor

Why Do We Have Creeds?

Burk Parsons

P&R
PUBLISHING
P.O. BOX 817 • PHILLIPSBURG • NEW JERSEY 08865-0817

Italics within Scripture quotations indicate emphasis added.

Page design by Tobias Design

Printed in the United States of America

Library of Congress Cataloging-in-Publication Data

Parsons, Burk.
Why do we have creeds? / Burk Parsons. -- 1st ed.
p. cm. -- (Basics of the faith)
Includes bibliographical references.
ISBN 978-1-59638-202-2 (pbk.)
1. Creeds. I. Title.
BT990.P377 2012
238--dc23

2011047696

Be not ashamed of your faith; remember it is the ancient gospel of the martyrs, confessors, reformers, and saints. Above all, it is the truth of God, against which all the gates of Hell cannot prevail. Let your lives adorn your faith, let your example adorn your creed.

—Foreword to the Baptist Confession of Faith (1689)

"I believe." We hear these words every day of our lives. Whatever the context, we use these two simple words to express our thoughts about nearly everything. When we want to tell others what we are thinking or want to reveal the innermost affections of our hearts, we will often say, "I believe." In his wisdom God created us not only with the capacity to believe, but also with an insatiable desire to explore, examine, and express our beliefs (Prov. 2; 1 Peter 1). We possess a God-given hunger deep within our souls that causes us to examine fundamental truths about everything God has revealed to us (Deut. 4; Matt. 22).

The mere fact that we believe in *something* doesn't actually do anything for us. At the most basic level, a belief in *something* only provides us with the overwhelming sense that we're not alone and that something exists beyond us. Everyone has a capacity to believe in *something*, and in fact everyone actually does believe something (Acts 17). Although the cynical skeptic might say, "I believe in nothing," the simple point is that he *does* believe in something, and according to him that something is "nothing." But even the convinced skeptic knows that it is impossible to believe in absolutely nothing. If someone claims to believe in nothing, the truth of the matter is that he actually believes in everything that begins and ends with himself as the source and object of his self-fashioned, self-centered faith. He has an open mind about everything, which, contrary to popular opinion, is not a good thing. As C. S. Lewis comments, "An open mind, in questions that are not ultimate, is useful. But an open mind about ultimate foundations . . . is idiocy. If a man's mind is open on these things, let his mouth at least be shut."[1] Someone who has an open mind will uncritically allow any and all data, no matter how absurd, to enter his mind and feel at home because he has no filters—no criteria—to discern right from wrong, truth from falsehood, and even truth from half-truth (Prov. 1:22, 32). The open mind is an undiscerning open space, filled only with perceptions and inclinations.

In order for belief to have heart-changing and life-changing significance, it requires God as both its source and object (Ps. 68:26; 1 Cor. 2:5). As Christians we are new creatures in Jesus Christ, and the Holy Spirit has graciously ripped out our hard hearts of stone and given us new, spiritually pliable hearts so that we are now able to believe, confess, and proclaim the glorious and eternal truths of God's sacred Word (Luke 24:45). We are to be open-minded to anything and everything that God has revealed to us, and by necessity we are to be completely, albeit graciously, closed-minded to anything that contradicts what he has revealed. As Christians we believe, confess, and proclaim God's truth and nothing but God's truth. This is why we have creeds, so that with unwavering resolve we might stand firm in the faith once delivered to the saints—to the end that we and our children would believe, confess, and proclaim God's unchanging truth for his glory, for he is the source of everything we believe and, thus, his revelation is our creedal standard for all of faith and life.

WHY DO WE HAVE CREEDS?

We have creeds because everyone believes in something, and even more to the point, everyone believes in God. Even self-proclaimed atheists believe there is a God, by virtue of God's revelation about himself in creation and the fact that all people are created in his image, and thus we are left without any excuse whatsoever (Rom. 1:18–20). So-called atheists know full well there's a God; they just hate God and find it easier for their consciences simply to pretend he does not exist.[2] But, as we know, even demons believe God exists and rightly tremble (Mark 5:7; James 2:19).

If everyone believes in God, the question then follows: what do we believe *about* God? To answer the question is to confess, or declare, our creed. A creed is a statement that describes our beliefs. The English word *creed* is a cognate of the Latin word *credo*, which means, "I believe." Dating back to the late twelfth century, the word *credo* likely emerged from the compound *kerd-dhe*, which can be translated "to put one's heart," pointing out the nature of a creed as that which we believe from our hearts and confess with our mouths.

As Augustine of Hippo confessed in a prayer, our hearts are restless until they rest in God and, as creatures made in God's image, we inherently possess the heart-capacity to believe and will, by necessity, possess some sort of creed. Whether formal or informal, written or verbal, in one way or another we all have a creed that details our beliefs. Some of us have a formal, written creed we adhere to, while others have an informal, unwritten creed that can easily change and perhaps often does change.

We are creedal by our very nature and begin to form concepts of belief from the moment we are born. As we move from the formation of concepts to actual statements of belief, we are naturally inclined toward verbal and even written creedal formulations that express our beliefs and unite us with other people around truths to which we all agree to adhere. Consider, for instance, a young child whose biological inclination is to trust his mother and father for nourishment, comfort, and protection. As the child matures, his perceived ideas about his mother and father are proven time and time again to the point that his nonverbal expressions turn into babbling verbal expressions that later mature into formal words when a child says to his mother and father, "Mommy and daddy, I love you so much." As that same child learns to read and write, some of his first drawings might depict the entire family with words expressing sincere love and affection for his family—all creedal expressions of what that child holds to be true. Our children believe in their hearts they are loved, so they confess with their mouths they are loved and naturally want to proclaim their love to others. By God's design, the entire human race is creedal—before the fall and after the fall—and will be throughout eternity in the new heavens and new earth. So the real question is not whether we have creeds. Rather, the questions are, What do we believe in our creeds? What is the nature of our belief? What is the authority, usefulness, foundation, and purpose of our creeds?

DOCTRINE IS LIFE

In answering the question about what we believe in our creeds, we must first grasp what it means to believe. In our day, unlike in the days of generations past, we have a much too simplistic view of what it means to believe something. In the world today, many people use the word *believe* to describe their feelings about something or describe a fleeting wish or hopeful desire. But as we consider the word *belief*, or *faith*, in its fullest biblical sense, we see that the word implies God's gracious act of giving and our humble act of receiving and resting on him alone, which involves our entire being: heart, mind, and will.[3]

Although we use the word *belief* in conjunction with all areas of human experience, usually when we use the word it is in the context of religious belief. The word *religious*, however, and all its derivatives, has fallen on hard times recently due largely to its longtime inappropriate use among those who understood neither the true Christian religion nor the genuine relationship with Christ by faith alone on which all Christian doctrine is established. Thus, preferring to emphasize their personal relationship with Christ over and against the religion that comes as a necessary and appropriate consequence of that relationship, some Christians, with the best intentions, have relegated their faith to one area of life rather than allowing their faith to overflow into every area of life. But the overflow of faith is the essential nature of faith itself—to encompass all of life by acknowledging, affirming, and applying the Christian doctrine we believe, confess, and proclaim. In the New Testament, James (1:22–25) repudiates the "worthless" religion of those who are merely "hearers" of the Word without being actual "doers" of the Word.

> If anyone thinks he is religious and does not bridle his tongue but deceives his heart, this person's religion is worthless. Religion that is pure and undefiled before God, the Father, is this: to visit orphans and widows in their affliction, and to keep oneself unstained from the world. (James 1:26–27)

James' point is simple—if our mouths (v. 26) and our lives (v. 22) do not demonstrate the authenticity of pure and undefiled religion, then we are simply deceiving ourselves and deceiving our hearts (vv. 22, 26).[4]

While it's certainly easy to understand why some use the word *religion* in a pejorative way, we must be careful to use words in their appropriate contexts in accordance with their historical definitions. Even Charles Spurgeon often used the word *religion* in an appropriate way to describe the all-encompassing Christian faith and life. In a sermon on Deuteronomy 32:47, "For it is not a vain thing for you; because it is your life" (KJV), Spurgeon criticized the merely outward, ceremonially superstitious religions of men (as did the apostle Paul in Acts 17), but then went on to employ the word *religion* positively when he said, "But with all these allowances, we still this morning assert most positively that the religion of Christ Jesus, that which has been revealed to us of the Holy Ghost by the apostles and prophets, and specially by the Messiah himself, when truly received into the heart, is no vain thing."[5] In the best and most appropriate sense of the word, *religion* is a helpful word we can use to describe our faith, which encompasses every aspect of our Christian lives, rooted in and flowing out of our spiritually regenerated new hearts and minds and established on the relationship that God has established with us.

In the fourth century Augustine advocated using the Latin word *religio* by highlighting its etymology *re-ligare*, which means "to join together" or "to bind together" as in a covenant bond between man and God.[6] The word *religion*, rightly understood, joins together everything we believe as we live it out in all of life. Furthermore, if we consider the lexical definitions of the word *religion*, we observe that *religion* describes not only a person's system of belief but also what a person practices, observes, and devotes himself to. As Herman Bavinck writes, "Religion must not just be *something* in one's life, but *everything*. Jesus demands that we love God with all our heart, all our soul, and all our strength."[7]

When the sixteenth-century pastor John Calvin wrote an all-encompassing systematic theology of the Christian faith, he titled his work, in Latin, *Institutio Christianae Religionis*, which can be translated *Institutes of Christian Religion*, or *Institutes of Christian Piety*. For Calvin a man's doctrine is the foundation of his entire religion, and a man's religion is not isolated to one segment of his life but has implications for all of life. We cannot restrict our doctrine as many attempt to do. Rather, our doctrine will, by its very nature, branch out into every sphere of Christian piety and practice. In other words, a man's doctrine is a man's life.

What we believe inescapably influences what we think, what we do, and even our motives of why and how we think it and do it. Those Christians who try to isolate their doctrine to their intellects so that it doesn't interfere with their daily lives are attempting the impossible. Either they do not possess true faith in Christ alone, or they will find that their doctrine refuses to be confined and instead begins to spread into all of life—from their hearts, to their souls, to their minds, and with all their strength. Mark Dever points out that if our religion is genuine it will naturally affect everything, including our care for others: "If our religion is real, if our faith is saving, it not only affects our actions, but affects our actions towards others. . . . Real religion cannot remain simply a 'vertical thing' between me and God. It must affect the way I deal with others."[8]

Christian doctrine, by its very nature, is an all-encompassing religion established on the entire system of doctrine, piety, and practice set forth in Scripture itself.[9] It is crucial that we grasp this if we are to understand the nature of creeds, our use of creeds, and the church's need for creeds. If we fail to see the all-encompassing nature of Christian doctrine, we certainly will not see the all-encompassing nature of creeds, which exist not only to affirm, confess, and proclaim the elementary matters of our faith, but to set forth the entirety of the doctrine, piety, and practice of the Christian religion.

DOCTRINE THAT DEMANDS OUR HEART, OUR LIFE, OUR ALL

As Christians, we must not only affirm our creedal doctrine with a perfunctory lip service or a mere intellectual assent, we must know our doctrine with our minds and believe our doctrine to the core of our being. This is necessary so that with a good and sincere conscience we might affirm and apply the truths of our creeds as we seek to fulfill our chief end, namely, to glorify God and enjoy him forever.[10]

In the eternal and covenantal religion that our triune God established with us his people, he necessarily and graciously provided a religion we would embrace and own in every part of our being, rooted within and flowing out of the heart, which is the central organ of the soul. In his *Summary of Christian Doctrine* Louis Berkhof writes the following concerning the "seat of religion":

> There are several wrong views respecting the seat of religion in man. Some think of religion primarily as a sort of knowledge, and locate it in the intellect. Others regard it as a kind of immediate feeling of God, and find its seat in the feelings. And still others hold that it consists most of all in moral activity, and refer it to the will. However, all these views are one-sided and contrary to Scripture, which teaches us that religion is a matter of the heart. In Scripture psychology the heart is the central organ of the soul. Out of it are all the issues of life, thoughts, feelings, and desires, Prov. 4:23. Religion involves the whole man, his intellectual, his emotional, and his moral life. This is the only view that does justice to the nature of religion.[11]

In much the same way, when the Bible speaks of belief, it speaks of our trust in our triune God who has provided us with a gloriously comprehensive faith that informs and transforms the heart—the representative living nucleus of our entire being.[12]

Several years ago when my wife and I began to teach our children the basics of the faith, we started with Jesus' summary of the Law: "You shall love the Lord your God with all your heart and with all your soul and with all your mind. This is the great and first commandment. And a second is like it: You shall love your neighbor as yourself" (Matt. 22:37–39). Before they learned anything more at the feet of Jesus, it was our foremost desire to teach our children that love for the Lord, including faith in the Lord, involves all aspects of our being—heart, soul, mind, and strength—and affects our relations with others and our love for others, even our enemies. What's more, we want our children to understand that knowing biblical doctrine, though foundational, is not an end in itself, but rather that by necessity, a true knowledge of biblical doctrine comes from God, teaches us about God, and leads us back to God in repentance, faith, and worship.[13]

In a similar fashion, J. C. Ryle warns against a mere intellectual knowledge of the Bible.

> Let us beware of an unsanctified knowledge of Christianity. It is a dangerous possession, but a fearfully common one in these latter days. We may know the Bible intellectually, and have no doubt about the truth of its contents. We may have our memories well stored with its leading texts, and be able to talk glibly about its leading doctrines. And all the time the Bible may have no influence over our hearts, and wills, and consciences. We may, in reality, be nothing better than the devils.[14]

The only way we can have a genuine, sanctified knowledge of God's Word is by the gracious and illuminating work of the Holy Spirit by the gospel of Jesus Christ, which is the power of God unto salvation to everyone who believes (Rom. 1:16). Such spiritually sanctified knowledge will establish what we believe about God and, in turn, what we believe about God will manifest itself in an all-encompassing religion that affects everything we believe, confess, and proclaim. However, when we say our belief about God affects everything, we are not only referring to our beliefs about God's attributes but our beliefs about all of God's revelation to us in his holy Word, the Scriptures of the Old and New Testaments, which are the foundation and fountain of our entire religion.

When we understand that Scripture is all-encompassing by its very nature, only then will we understand that all of

Scripture is our rule for all of faith and life. In opposition to contemporary Roman Catholic dogma, and in agreement with the Protestant Reformers of the sixteenth century, we not only affirm *sola Scriptura* (Scripture alone) as our final authority, but we also affirm *tota Scriptura* (Scripture in total—all of Scripture) as our final authority in its canonical entirety. As a result, we must seek Scripture's authority so that we might fully acknowledge, affirm, and apply all its truths as our only infallible guide for faith and all of life.

THE NECESSITY OF SCRIPTURE ALONE

Our belief about God informs every other belief. And while God has revealed himself generally in creation, it is only what God has revealed specially to us in his Word that guides us finally and infallibly—without error. God gave us himself and everything that comes with knowing him, which entails knowledge of ourselves and others, of sin and salvation, of life and death, of Satan and our Savior.[15] His Word is our only infallible guide, and from it we obtain true and saving knowledge about our all-encompassing religion. As such, it is from God's Word alone that we derive the doctrine that informs us and that, in turn, must inform our creeds.

Scott Clark explains how we must constantly submit our doctrinal presuppositions about Scripture to Scripture itself as our final authority: "Christian theology must be driven by the Scriptures, but no one reads the Scripture without a theology. So we must be constantly submitting our theology, that is, our understanding of Scripture, to the Scriptures themselves for revision and correction."[16] And while the Bible and theology can never be separated, we distinguish them and thereby strive to ensure that our theology is constantly being formed and reformed according to Scripture. Alister McGrath offers a helpful explanation of the relationship between doctrine and God's revelation.

> Doctrine is our effort to articulate what He has made known. Doctrine is the divinely authorized attempt to describe God in accordance with how He has revealed Himself in creation, in history, in Jesus Christ and in the Scriptures. In doing so, doctrine also serves to expose false interpretations of reality, false concepts of God. It is the aim of doctrine to make sense of the individual's and the church's experience of God as He has made Himself known in Jesus Christ.[17]

If our doctrine is right doctrine, then it is established on and will necessarily be directed by and informed by Scripture, which is the only true, special revelation from the one and only true God. False religions do not have doctrine but mere speculative manmade theories about the one true God of the one true Word. Consequently, our natural, God-given desire to formulate what we believe can only rightly be formulated by looking to the supernatural, God-given source, which is nothing more and nothing less than sacred Scripture. A. A. Hodge explains it this way:

> The Scriptures of the Old and New Testament having been given by inspiration of God, are for man in his present state the only and the all-sufficient rule of faith and practice. This divine word, therefore, is the only standard of doctrine which has any intrinsic authority binding the consciences of men. All other standards are of value or authority only as they teach what the Scriptures teach.[18]

It would seem appropriate then for us to conclude that the Bible is all we really need. Since God saw fit to provide us with Scripture as our only infallible guide for faith and life, it necessarily follows that Scripture is completely sufficient to serve as the final, incontrovertible judge and standard of our beliefs. Right? Without a doubt—all we need is God's Word. That's precisely what God himself teaches us (John 17:17; 2 Tim. 3:16; 2 Peter 3:16). So, then, what about the historic creeds of our faith, such as the Apostles' Creed or the Nicene Creed? And what about all the Reformed confessions and catechisms of the sixteenth and seventeenth centuries, such as the Westminster Confession of Faith or the Heidelberg Catechism? If Scripture alone is profitable for teaching, reproof, correction, and training in righteousness to the end that we would be competent and equipped for every good work, then why do we need anything else? If the Lord God Almighty wanted us to have anything beyond the sixty-six books of sacred Scripture, could he not have simply provided it to us? Are creeds and confessions really needed in the life of the Christian and in the life of the church? Samuel Miller, in his classic work *The Utility and Importance of Creeds and Confessions*, puts it this way:

> But still it is asked—"Where is the need of any definitive declaration of what we understand the scriptures to teach? Are they not intelligible enough in themselves? Can we make them plainer than their Author has done? Why hold a candle to the sun? Why make an attempt to frame a more explicit test than He who gave the Bible has thought proper to frame—an attempt, as vain as it is presumptuous?"[19]

These are necessary and inescapable questions that every Christian must consider when it comes to creeds.

And we can easily see how such questions extend not only to creeds but to the nature and purpose of the study of doctrine itself. What's more, such questions extend naturally to any and all study of Scripture—all commentaries, all systematic theologies, all sermons, and all discussions and disputes about anything in the Bible. Any time someone considers for a moment what God has revealed, he has begun to formulate a creed. Whenever we sing simple songs to our children, such as "Jesus loves me, this I know, for the Bible tells me so," we have formulated a creedal statement about Jesus, his love, the object of his love, our assurance of his love, and the nature of biblical authority.

Still, some might say, "My only creed is Christ." But as soon as we ask the question, "Who is Christ?" we will hear someone's expression of his creedal understanding about Christ, which will be either right or wrong, biblical or unbiblical.[20] And an unbiblical belief about the person and work of Christ will result in our condemnation. For if it is the Christ of the Bible who unites us, we must affirm the one, true biblical Christ in order to have true biblical salvation and true biblical unity. Thus, it would be quite appropriate to say, "My only creed is the creed of Christ." This is the aim of every Christian, namely, to believe, confess, and proclaim the very creed and doctrine of Scripture that Christ himself authored, fulfills, defends, and proclaims. If we are genuine Christians who trust Christ alone, it is impossible for us not to affirm the elementary saving doctrine of Christ our Lord and Savior; the only question is whether or not the entirety of our doctrine is sound doctrine or false doctrine. R. C. Sproul writes, "To the Christian, doctrine is unavoidable. Ours is never a choice between doctrine and no doctrine, but between sound doctrine and false doctrine. This is nowhere more urgent than when we are talking about the Christ, who is the object of our faith."[21]

THE AUTHORITY OF SCRIPTURE AND THE AUTHORITY OF CREEDS

The church's historic creeds affirm that Scripture alone is our final authority. The Westminster Standards (consisting of the Westminster Confession of Faith, the Westminster Larger Catechism, and the Westminster Shorter Catechism) affirm that the sixty-six-book canon of Scripture is "given by inspiration of God to be the rule of faith and life."[22] The London Baptist Confession of Faith states it this way at the very outset: "The Holy Scripture is the only sufficient, certain, and infallible rule of all saving knowledge, faith, and obedience."[23] In essence, the church's creeds and confessions themselves affirm that the church's creeds and confessions of faith do not stand as authorities over Scripture but rather serve as affirmations of Scripture's authority for all of faith and life. Again, Sproul explains, "Creedal statements are an attempt to show a coherent and unified understanding of the whole scope of Scripture."[24]

Creeds themselves are authoritative only in that they are subordinate to and derivative from the only divine authority, namely, the inspired and inerrant Word of God. As is the case with pastors, popes, and churches, creeds cannot create new revelation, invent new teachings, or make new laws to bind the consciences of God's people. Creeds serve to affirm the authority of God's Word, not to stand alone as authorities unto themselves. Creeds are formulated and subscribed to as if they were theological mirrors of the Bible's fundamental doctrine. As such, creeds exist to summarily reflect the truth, not to advance new truths. Moreover, the simple fact of the matter is that there is no such thing as "new truth," for if something is actually true, it is not new, and if something is actually new, it certainly is not true. Truth isn't created by man, but only learned from God. Creeds merely serve to reflect and affirm, by way of systematic summary, the unchanging truth of God for the people of God.

In his helpful work *Credo*, Jaroslav Pelikan draws attention to the reciprocal nature of our reasoning as we look to creeds that, in turn, point back to Scripture as our final authority. Creeds are, he writes, "pointing beyond themselves . . . in what very much looks like an argument in a circle. . . . The Scripture is to be understood as the tradition and this particular creed interpret it, but this particular creed, as well as perhaps the tradition, is subject to the Scripture."[25] What Pelikan points out drives us again to this fundamental question: If creeds do not teach us anything new, and if creeds exist simply to affirm what Scripture teaches, how are creeds useful?

THE USEFULNESS OF CREEDS

To answer the question in part, it may be helpful to think of creeds as maps, or guides, to help us navigate our way as we study God's Word, looking to the doctrinal map keys formulated by our forefathers. While someone could argue that we don't really need maps in order to travel, we all know how helpful maps are if we want to arrive at a particular destination on a particular route in a particular amount of time. G. I. Williamson writes,

> The Bible contains a great wealth of information. It isn't easy to master it all—in fact, no one has ever mastered it completely. It would therefore be foolish for us to try to do it on our own, starting from scratch. We would be ignoring all the study of the

> Word of God that other people have done down through the centuries. That is exactly why we have creeds. They are the product of many centuries of Bible study by a great company of believers. They are a kind of spiritual "road map" of the teaching of the Bible, already worked out and proved by others before us.[26]

We use maps whenever we need assistance getting to a particular destination that is not familiar to us, but we do not typically look at a map of a road we have traveled often because we have committed that route to memory. But unless we travel to a particular destination regularly, we can lose our way and wander off the most convenient route because our minds do not think as clearly or remember as fully as we would like. The Bible is a beautiful and vast world of mountains, rivers, and paths, and we are called to climb them, navigate them, and walk them as we look to, learn from, and lean on those who have traveled them faithfully in generations past.

Still, someone could easily level the charge against the usefulness of creeds by pointing out that our forefathers, though faithful, were sinners and therefore disqualified from formulating creeds for the church. There is a two-fold response to this charge. First, after our fall into sin, God has continued to call, gift, and equip redeemed and repentant sinners to serve him and his called-out people, the church, to the end that God's people would believe, confess, and proclaim his truth. Second, as redeemed and repentant sinners who are naturally inclined to formulate creeds, we must grasp that it is our sin itself that leads us to disagree, dispute, and divide within the church, which is precisely what God himself commands against in his Word. So, while we can conclude that it is because of sin that we are naturally inclined toward differing beliefs, it is also because of sin that we should strive diligently to formulate a written creed that affirms the doctrine of Scripture. More to the point, however, our sin has not only affected us by dividing us as the one body of Christ, it has also degenerated our minds within us as individual members of the body of Christ. The nineteenth-century Presbyterian pastor Robert Lewis Dabney writes, "As man's mind is notoriously fallible, and professed Christians who claim to hold the Scriptures, as they understand them, differ from each other notoriously, some platform for union and cooperation must be adopted, by which those who believe they are truly agreed may stand and work together."[27] As such, on account of the noetic[28] effects of sin, our minds do not function this side of heaven as they were originally created to function. In addition to thinking unclearly, we do not remember as well as we should. Simply put, because of the effects of sin on our minds we need all the help we can get in thinking about and remembering all that God has revealed to us, both for our own sake and for the sake of our children. Is it not then a matter of wisdom to have written creeds that clearly and concisely summarize the Bible's system of doctrine, that we might better learn and teach others the fundamentals of the Christian religion?

Even as spiritually regenerate believers, we suffer the noetic effects of sin and do not always think as clearly and as carefully as we should when we study Scripture. However, in his grace God has given us his Spirit, and in his wisdom he has given us pastors and teachers until Christ's consummation of his kingdom. The Holy Spirit illumines his Word to us and leads in the truth of his Word as he enables and employs his servants to study, explain, and teach his truth in sermons, Bible study lessons, commentaries, books, and creeds. So creeds, similar to sermons, are written, formulated explanations meant to provide us with a clear summary of the doctrine of Scripture.

Not only does sin cloud our thinking, it clouds our memories. We do not always remember as fully and as quickly as we should from our study of Scripture, which is why God himself has given us creedal summaries of his Word throughout his Word.[29] And just like the concise creed-like statements in Scripture, the church's historic creeds provide us with a concise system of the doctrine of Scripture so that we might better and more easily learn and remember the doctrine our Lord has revealed to us in his Word.

Without sin just about everything would be different, and we would not have any need whatsoever for creeds. If we were not sinners, we would all read and believe God's Word exactly as God intended. We would not disagree about anything in Scripture. There would be no divisions in the church. There would be no false teachers, no heresy, and no need for church discipline. The one, holy, catholic (universal), and apostolic church would completely agree on everything. And such will be the reality in the new heavens and new earth. But alas, we are sinners with depraved hearts and debauched minds as a result of the often-underestimated fall of man into sin, which put us at enmity not only with God but also, to a lesser degree, with one another. We must not undervalue the consequences of sin. Rather, we must have a high regard for the depravity of man and for the overwhelming effects of sin on all we think, say, and do, and on the motives behind all we think, say, and do. Consequently, it's precisely because each and every one of us is a sinner and because there is more than one of us that, by necessity, we need creeds. Samuel Miller writes, "If every Christian were a mere insulated individual, who inquired, felt, and acted for himself alone, no creed of human formation would be necessary for his advancement in knowledge, comfort, or holiness."[30]

Contrary to popular opinion, we have creeds not to divide us but to unite us on the foundational beliefs of the one and only true faith. Doctrine doesn't divide, nor do creeds. Sin is what divides us, and doctrine is what unites us. Through our union with Christ and by the illuminating power of the Holy Spirit in God's Word, our affirmation of biblical doctrine is the only thing that can possibly unite a church comprised of self-confessed, repentant sinners. In an article on creeds, Tom Nettles quotes Southern Baptist minister B. H. Carrol to argue the importance of creeds for the true unity and liberty of the church: "The modern cry, 'less creed and more liberty,' is a degeneration from the vertebrate to the jellyfish, and it means more heresy. Definitive truth does not create heresy—it only exposes and corrects. Shut off the creed and the Christian world would fill up with heresy unsuspected and uncorrected, but nonetheless deadly."[31] It is the ignorance and denial of truth that divides and destroys, but it is the knowledge and affirmation of truth that unites and brings genuine purity and lasting peace. Robert Lewis Dabney explains further, "Such a creed, instead of being a cause of schism, is an *irenicum* [a proposal for promoting peace], a source of mutual respect, brotherly love and substantial agreement, amidst minor differences, between the several branches of the church catholic."[32]

The more we know the doctrine of Scripture, the more we will find ourselves visibly united to one another through the uniting power of the gospel as the one, holy, catholic, and apostolic church of Jesus Christ. In their book *The Deliberate Church*, Mark Dever and Paul Alexander write, "When the Gospel enables us to live in love, even though we may have nothing else in common save Christ, it is a testimony to its power to transform a group of sinful, self-centered people into a loving community united by a common relationship with Jesus Christ."[33] This is precisely what the apostle Paul teaches us. In his letter to the Ephesians, writing in order to more fully explain the revealed mystery of our salvation and the identity of who we are as the body of Christ, the church, Paul writes,

> There is one body and one Spirit—just as you were called to the one hope that belongs to your call—one Lord, one faith, one baptism, one God and Father of all, who is over all and through all and in all. (Eph. 4:4–6)

THE FOUNDATION FOR CREEDS

We should all be familiar with the Great Commission that Jesus gave his disciples before he ascended to the right hand of God the Father Almighty, but in my experience as a pastor I have found that many Christians are not as familiar with it as they should be. Typically I find that the Great Commission is reduced solely to a call to evangelism. And while it is indeed a call to evangelism, it is not only a call to evangelism but a command to go and make disciples of all nations, which includes baptizing and teaching, and as D. A. Carson explains, "baptizing and teaching characterize" disciple making.[34] Let us carefully consider what Jesus teaches in the Great Commission as recorded for us in Matthew 28:18–20.

> All authority in heaven and on earth has been given to me. Go therefore and make disciples of all nations, baptizing them in the name of the Father and of the Son and of the Holy Spirit, teaching them to observe all that I have commanded you. And behold, I am with you always, to the end of the age.

When we consider or discuss the Great Commission we usually and rightly emphasize Jesus' primary verbal command, "Go and make disciples of all nations." Sometimes we include the first participial phrase, "baptizing them in the name of the Father and of the Son and of the Holy Spirit." However, we often fail to emphasize not only the second participle, but the entirety of the phrase as well: "teaching them to observe all that I have commanded you." To be faithful to the Great Commission is to be faithful to it entirely, which means that we should not only go and make disciples, but we should also baptize and teach all that Jesus commanded until he returns, that all his people might know him and worship him, now and forever.

We must not forget that as our primary and supreme comforter, Jesus did not leave us alone when he ascended but promised there would be another comforter, or helper, namely, the Holy Spirit. "I will ask the Father, and he will give you another Helper, to be with you forever" (John 14:16). In that same conversation with his disciples Jesus went on to explain further what the Holy Spirit would do. "The Helper, the Holy Spirit, whom the Father will send in my name, he will teach you all things and bring to your remembrance all that I have said to you" (John 14:26). There is a common thread that runs throughout these two passages in the gospel accounts. In both his Great Commission (Matt. 28) and in his final discourse in the upper room (John 13–17), Jesus promises to provide us with sustaining comfort as we teach and are taught all things. What the Son of God commands in the Great Commission the Spirit of God supplies as he guides us "into all the truth" (John 16:13). As he indwells us, the Holy Spirit teaches us through the very means that he himself has not only permitted, but through the means of men he has called and gifted for the church today, namely, pastors and teachers (Eph. 4:11). In his sovereign wisdom God has not only given us his truth by his grace, but he has given us the means to learn his truth as we, by his grace, strive to believe, confess, and proclaim his truth fully and entirely. Paul describes this in Ephesians 4, making perhaps the most poignant biblical case for the necessity of creeds.

> And he gave the apostles, the prophets, the evangelists, the shepherds and teachers, to equip the saints for the work of ministry, for building up the body of Christ, until we all attain to the unity of the faith and of the knowledge of the Son of God, to mature manhood, to the measure of the stature of the fullness of Christ, so that we may no longer be children, tossed to and fro by the waves and carried about by every wind of doctrine, by human cunning, by craftiness in deceitful schemes. Rather, speaking the truth in love, we are to grow up in every way into him who is the head, into Christ, from whom the whole body, joined and held together by every joint with which it is equipped, when each part is working properly, makes the body grow so that it builds itself up in love (Eph. 4:11–16).

What Paul explains to the growing, world-advancing church at Ephesus is precisely what Jesus teaches in the Great Commission as he commends to us an all-encompassing faith and life that is consumed with learning to "observe" all that Jesus commanded us as his disciples at his feet and disciple makers to the nations. Simply put, to observe all Jesus' teaching we must believe, confess, and proclaim his truth in all our doctrine, piety, and practice, not as "children tossed to and fro by the waves and carried about by every wind of doctrine" but as mature disciples of Jesus Christ standing firm on the doctrine of Scripture. In order to do this we must strive to learn and remember the entirety of the doctrine of Scripture that Jesus himself affirmed, confessed, and proclaimed. As sinful creatures, the best way we know to do this is to search Scripture as the Bereans did (Acts 17), collectively affirm what Scripture teaches as the council at Jerusalem did (Acts 15), and declare it and disseminate it in every way possible as the apostles did (Acts 15:22–34), using a format by which we can more easily learn and remember, just like Paul did wherever he went (Acts 15:30; 19:8; 26:23).

During the first century, as the apostles and other elders were forced to combat false teaching that strayed from sound doctrine, the church found it necessary to have creedal statements in order to guard against outright heresy. The church formulated miniature creeds to help preserve the doctrine of Scripture—in order to preserve souls from death. The apostle Paul provides us with many examples of such creeds that are like biblically sown seeds in the rich soil of the early church—seeds that grew into the more-advanced creedal formulations of the church in subsequent centuries. Among the creed-like formulations of the apostle Paul (Rom. 10:9; 1 Cor. 15:3–7; Phil. 2:6–11; Col. 1:15–20), his words in his first letter to Timothy are perhaps the most succinct for our purpose here.

> Great indeed, we confess, is the mystery of godliness:
>
> He was manifested in the flesh,
> vindicated by the Spirit,
> seen by angels,
> proclaimed among the nations,
> believed on in the world,
> taken up in glory. (1 Tim. 3:16)

The concise nature of Paul's words of confession to Timothy serve as a good example of something we see throughout Scripture; for example, the Ten Commandments (Ex. 20), the Shema (Deut. 6), John's summary of the gospel (John 3:16), and Paul's formulation of his gospel message (1 Cor. 15:3–7). Throughout the apostolic era and afterward, as the effects of sin continued to yield false teachers and their false teaching, and as new heresies were invented, the people of God found it necessary and prudent to reaffirm the sound doctrine of Scripture. Much like the church's creeds through the centuries, the creeds of the apostolic era and the early church were formulated to serve the church as God spiritually matured his body and advanced his kingdom throughout the world.

So whether we have in mind the only inspired and infallible creedal formulations in Scripture itself or the uninspired and fallible creedal formulations such as the Apostles' Creed, the Nicene Creed,[35] the London Baptist Confession of Faith, the Three Forms of Unity of the Dutch Reformed churches consisting of the Heidelberg Catechism, Canons of Dordt, and Second Belgic Confession, or the confessional standards to which I heartily subscribe, the Westminster Confession of Faith and Catechisms, it is crucial that we understand the church's God-given duty to be a faithful steward and guardian of the one and only faith delivered to the saints in order to provide the church of all generations with carefully worded, concise summaries of the doctrine of Scripture.

THE PURPOSE OF CREEDS

Throughout the ages creeds have come under attack on numerous occasions, and such attacks have come almost exclusively from heretics outside the church, which, incidentally, ought to tell us something. Even today at the beginning of the twenty-first century there seems to be a disregard, albeit even disdain, for creeds, not to mention a growing ignorance of creeds even among those who profess to subscribe to them. With this in mind, I offer an apologetic of sorts for the formulation, usefulness, and purpose of the church's creeds and confessions. Though by no means exhaustive, I offer this list to provide the church with a practical ten-point summary of the purpose of creeds in the church, in no particular order.

The purpose of creeds is

1. To *glorify* God according to his truth and to enjoy him forever by believing, confessing, and proclaiming our doctrine in accordance with what he has revealed and not according to the superstitions of men, the deceitful schemes of Satan, or the arrogant and presumptuous notions of our own hearts.
2. To *affirm* the one true God almighty who has revealed himself to us and whose glorious attributes, gracious laws, and grand story of redemption point us to himself as our only Lord to the end that we might love him rightly and as fully as possible with all our heart, with all our soul, with all our mind, and with all our strength.
3. To *guard* the unchanging, sound doctrine of Scripture against false teachers and heretics outside the church, and to guard against the vain and false notions of Scripture from within the church as a shining witness of God's truth to the watching world out of which God calls his elect through the preaching of the gospel and inward call of the Holy Spirit.
4. To *discern* truth from doctrinal error and to discern truth from half-truth as we contend earnestly for

the faith once delivered to the saints that we might grow up in every way into Christ, who is the living head of the church, who is the way, the truth, the life, and the only way to the Father.

5. To *remain* steadfast through the ages until Christ's return as one, holy, catholic, and apostolic church of Christ who believe, confess, and proclaim the pure and unadulterated Word of God and who rightly administer the sacraments of baptism and the Lord's Supper, including our consistent exercise of church admonition, correction, and discipline.
6. To *uphold* the life-encompassing doctrine of the inspired and inerrant Word of God as our sole, infallible authority that is profitable for doctrine, for reproof, for correction, for instruction in righteousness to the end that every man of God might be complete, thoroughly equipped for every good work.
7. To *maintain* freedom for individual Christians as well as the entire church from extra-biblical laws, traditions, and superstitions of men that bind men's consciences, perplex men's souls, lead our children astray according to their sin, and bring about man-exalting pride instead of God-exalting humility.
8. To *confirm* men according to the church's doctrinal standard who have been elected to serve as officers of the church as well as to equip, examine, and prove those men who have been called as pastors and elders over the flock of God, and to ascertain their suitability to teach as they feed, care for, and pray with and for the sheep of Christ for whom he gave his life.
9. To *preserve* the purity and, thereby, the peace and unity of the church visible as the outward witness of Christ and his elect bride, the church invisible, to the end

that we might stand together as one family with one Father, one Lord, one faith, one baptism, unwaveringly according to and because of the truth, never in spite of, disregard for, or ignorance of it.

10. To *fulfill* the Great Commission in our united affirmation and proclamation of the one true gospel of Jesus Christ, which is the only power of God unto salvation to all who believe, by making disciples in our homes, churches, communities, and in all nations, baptizing them in the name of the Father, Son, and Holy Spirit and teaching them to observe all things that our Lord Jesus Christ commanded us.

UNITED IN GOD'S TRUTH FOR GOD'S GLORY

In 1626, Lutheran pastor Peter Meiderlin wrote a treatise to his fellow pastors who, at the time, were entrenched in controversies with those outside the Lutheran church and involved in spirited contentions with one another. He wrote to remind his fellow gospel ministers of the doctrinal unity that existed among them because of their shared Lutheran creed, The Book of Concord (1580). In his treatise, he gleaned from the church's faithful forefathers down through the ages as he wrote what has become one of the most oft-quoted maxims in church history to this day, "*In necessarriis, unitas; in dubiis, libertas; in omnibus, caritas*," or "in essentials, unity; in non-essentials, liberty; in all things, charity (love)." Because they affirmed the essential, primary doctrines of the faith, they were able to enjoy authentic unity within their Lutheran assembly of ministers and maintain a certain degree of ecclesial unity and fellowship with those of other traditions, such as the Reformed

Calvinists and Scottish Presbyterians, and other movements with the Lutheran tradition, such as German Pietism. They had unity not in spite of the truth but precisely because of the truth and because of their adherence to the truth in their respective creeds, which affirmed, confessed, and proclaimed the fundamental doctrine of Scripture.

The same is true today. As Christians from different Bible-believing denominations within the Protestant Reformed tradition, we disagree on numerous matters that we sincerely believe are important, biblical matters. Naturally, we will contend over these secondary matters to win our brothers to those doctrinal positions and exegetical interpretations we believe to be biblically accurate. As J. Gresham Machen reasons, "In the sphere of religion, as in other spheres, the things about which men are agreed are apt to be the things that are least worth holding; the really important things are the things about which men will fight."[36]

While there are certainly differences among us, it is because of the existence of our stated beliefs, that is, our formal, written creeds, that we are able to maintain unity grounded in the essential matters of salvation and show liberty on matters not essential to the church's fundamental doctrines. Meanwhile we maintain our gospel bond with biblically informed and truth-motivated love, recognizing the importance of each and every matter of God's Word. Reflecting on this, the great twentieth-century British preacher D. Martyn Lloyd-Jones commented, "We must be very careful to draw this distinction between essentials and non-essentials lest we become guilty of schism and begin to rend the body of Christ."[37]

Although many have used Peter Meiderlin's words about unity in order to try to achieve ecumenical unity by way of doctrinal compromise, his words cannot rightly be used for such a purpose, for they drive us not away from doctrinal and creedal precision but directly toward it for the sake of genuine unity, liberty, and charity in the church whose infallible guide for faith and life is Scripture alone.[38] What is so amazing about the church's historic creeds is not their doctrinal differences, which certainly do exist, but the overwhelming doctrinal agreement among them. Indeed, the unity of the church is proven not through doctrinal compromise, declared peace, or perceived unity in spite of our secondary and tertiary doctrinal differences, even though all our differences are important. Rather, the unity of the church is proven in our affirmation, confession, and proclamation of the fundamental doctrinal matters of our one Christian religion, without which unity we stand not within the church but remain outside the one and only church of God.[39] This creedal unity is rooted in God's revealed truth, which comes to us as a direct result of God's love for us, which, in turn, manifests itself in our affirmed, confessed, and proclaimed love for each other as a witness to the watching world. Puritan pastor Thomas Watson goes further: "There is but one God, and they that serve Him should be one. There is nothing that would render the true religion more lovely, or make more proselytes to it, than to see the professors of it tied together with the heart-strings of love."[40] This, after all, is what Jesus taught us when he said, "A new commandment I give to you, that you love one another: just as I have loved you, you also are to love one another. By this all people will know that you are my disciples, if you have love for one another" (John 13:34–35).

Although it is because of our sin that different creeds exist, it is for the sake of our love for each other, our love for the body of Christ as one, holy, catholic, and apostolic church, and our love for Christ himself that we must affirm, confess, and proclaim the unchanging doctrine of Scripture in our creeds, striving always for one united creed—the creed of Jesus Christ until he returns. And as the Holy Spirit sustains and enables us, it will be our fervent prayer that God's redeeming truth will be proclaimed in every home, church, and nation—transforming hearts, renewing minds, and encompassing the entirety of our lives by the power of the Holy Spirit as we love our neighbors as ourselves and love our Lord, glorifying and enjoying him forever with all our hearts.

NOTES

1 C. S. Lewis, *The Abolition of Man* (New York: HarperOne, 1974), 48.

2 As the one-time atheist C. S. Lewis admitted, "Atheists express their rage against God although in their view He does not exist." *The Problem of Pain* (New York: HarperCollins, 2011), 93.

3 The Westminster Larger Catechism (Q&A 72) answers "What is justifying faith?" this way, "Justifying faith is a saving grace, wrought in the heart of a sinner by the Spirit and Word of God, whereby he, being convinced of his sin and misery, and of the disability in himself and all other creatures to recover him out of his lost condition, not only assenteth to the truth of the promise of the gospel, but receiveth and resteth upon Christ and his righteousness, therein held forth, for pardon of sin, and for the accepting and accounting of his person righteous in the sight of God for salvation."

4 The word that James uses, translated rightly as "religion" is the Greek word *thréskos*, which means simply "pious" or "religious." However, the word the apostle Paul employs in Acts 17:22 sometimes, wrongly, translated "religious" is the Greek word *deisidaimonésteros* meaning "fear-driven superstition by a confused concept of God." Similarly, the word that Paul uses in Colossians 2:23 is the compound word *ethelothrēskeía*, properly translated as "self-willed religion," and thus not true God-willed religion.

5 C. H. Spurgeon, "Religion: A Reality," *Metropolitan Tabernacle Pulpit*, vol. 8 (1862).

6 Augustine, "Of True Religion," *Earlier Writings*, ed. J. H. S. Burleigh (Louisville, KY: Westminster John Knox Press, 2006), 282. Wayne Baker summarizes the word *religion* culling teaching from Heinrich Bullinger: "Two or more place themselves under obligations or bind themselves to conditions. Therefore Christianity was called *religio*, from *religare*, to bind. God made His covenant with the human race from the very beginning, binding himself to man and *agreeing to certain conditions* with us which He explained to the blessed patriarchs, such as Adam, Noah, Abraham, and Moses, revealing himself from time to time more and more, clarifying and renewing this covenant or testament." J. Wayne Baker, *Heinrich Bullinger and the Covenant* (Athens, OH: Ohio University Press, 1980), 76.

7 Herman Bavinck, "Philosophy of Religion (Faith)," *Essays on Religion, Science, and Society*, ed. John Bolt (Grand Rapids, MI: Baker Academic, 2008), 29–30.

8 Mark Dever, "Pure Religion," in *Tabletalk* (Sanford, FL: Ligonier Ministries, March 2005).

9 B. B. Warfield writes, "The revelations of the Scriptures do not terminate upon the intellect. They were given not merely to enlighten the mind. They were given through the intellect to beautify the life. They terminate on the heart. Again, they do not, in affecting the heart, leave the intellect untouched. They cannot be fully understood by the intellect, acting alone. . . . No man can intellectually grasp the full meaning of the revelations of authority, save as the result of an experience of their power in life." Benjamin B. Warfield, "Authority, Intellect, Heart," *Benjamin B. Warfield: Selected Shorter Writings*, vol. 1, ed. John Meeter (Phillipsburg, NJ: P&R, 2001), 671.

10 Ligon Duncan writes, "Until we cease to be satisfied with mere assent or acquiescence to whatever theological system of confession we propose, and begin to demand a personal embrace, belief, and owning of that confession . . . we will not be safe." As Duncan rightly exhorts, we must embrace and own our confession, or creed. J. Ligon Duncan III, "Owning the Confession: Subscription in the Scottish Presbyterian Tradition," *The Practice of Confessional Subscription*, ed. David Hall (Oakridge, TN: The Covenant Foundation, 1997), 88.

11 Louis Berkhof, *Summary of Christian Doctrine* (Grand Rapids, MI: Eerdmans, 1938), 10.

12 As G. C. Berkouwer writes, "The heart is not simply some single component of a biblical psychology. It is the seat of the whole person, it is his depth dimension, from which his full human existence is directed and formed." *Man: The Image of God*, Studies in Dogmatics (Grand Rapids, MI: Eerdmans, 1962), 203.

13 "Thomas Aquinas expressed himself as follows: *Theologia a Deo docetur, Deum docet, et ad Deum ducit*" ("Theology is taught by God, teaches God, and leads unto God"). Louis Berkhof, *Systematic Theology* (Grand Rapids, MI: Eerdmans, 1996), 390.

14 J. C. Ryle, *Expository Thoughts on Luke*, vol. 2 (Carlisle, PA: Banner of Truth, 1988), 125.

15 See John Calvin, *Institutes of the Christian Religion*, 1.1.1.

16 R. Scott Clark, *Recovering the Reformed Confession* (Phillipsburg, NJ: P&R, 2008), 201.

17 Alister McGrath, *Understanding Doctrine: Its Relevance and Purpose for Today* (Grand Rapids, MI: Zondervan, 1990), 43.

18 A. A. Hodge, "A Short History of Creeds and Confessions" in *The Confession of Faith* (Carlisle, PA: Banner of Truth, 1998), 1.

19 Samuel Miller, *The Utility and Importance of Creeds and Confessions* (Philadelphia, PA: Presbyterian Board of Publication, 1839), 21.

20 For example, the Disciples of Christ churches explicitly claim to have "no creed but Christ," yet are quick to refer to and disseminate their twenty-page document called "What We Believe."

21 Archie Parrish and R. C. Sproul, *The Spirit of Revival* (Wheaton, IL: Crossway, 2000), 31.

22 Westminster Confession of Faith 1.2.

23 London Baptist Confession of Faith (1689) 1.1.

24 R. C. Sproul, "Norma Normata—A Rule That Is Ruled," *Tabletalk* (Sanford, FL: Ligonier Ministries, April 2008).

25 Jaroslav Pelikan, *Credo* (New Haven, CT: Yale University Press, 2003), 127.

26 G. I. Williamson, *The Heidelberg Catechism: A Study Guide* (Phillipsburg, NJ: P&R, 1993), 2–3.

27 Robert Lewis Dabney, *Discussions*, vol. 1 (Richmond: Presbyterian Committee of Publication, 1890), 315.

28 The noetic effects of sin can be defined as the manner in which sin blinds, damages, and affects man's mind and intellect with respect to his grasp of spiritual truth, his knowledge of God, and his accurate knowledge of everything else.

29 See section "The Foundation for Creeds."

30 Miller, *The Utility and Importance of Creeds and Confessions*, 3.

31 Tom Nettles, "Missions and Creeds," *The Founders Journal*, vol. 17, September 1994.

32 Dabney, *Discussions*, vol. 5, 141.

33 Mark Dever and Paul Alexander, *The Deliberate Church* (Wheaton, IL: Crossway, 2005), 111.

34 D. A. Carson, *Matthew*, The Expositor's Bible Commentary, vol. 8, ed. Frank E. Gaebelein (Grand Rapids, MI: Zondervan), 597.

35 The creed commonly referred to today as the Nicene Creed is, technically speaking, the "Niceno-Constantinopolitan Creed" as it was formulated in part at Nicea in 325 and in its entirety at Constantinople in 381.

36 J. Gresham Machen, *Christianity and Liberalism* (Grand Rapids, MI: Eerdmans, 1923), 1–2.

37 D. Martyn Lloyd-Jones, *What Is an Evangelical?* (Carlisle, PA: Banner of Truth, 1992), 90.

38 John Calvin writes, "For not all the articles of true doctrine are of the same sort. Some are so necessary to know that they should be certain and unquestioned by all men as the proper principles of religion. Such are: God is one, Christ is God and the Son of God; our salvation rests in God's mercy; and the like. Among the churches there are other articles of doctrine disputed, which still do not break the unity of faith. Suppose that one church believes—short of unbridled contention and opinionated stubbornness—that souls upon leaving bodies fly to heaven; while another, not daring to define the place, is convinced nevertheless that they live to the Lord. What churches would disagree on this one point? Here are the apostle's words: 'Let us therefore, as many as are perfect, be of the same mind; and if you be differently minded in anything, God shall reveal this also to you' (Phil. 3:15). Does this not sufficiently indicate that a difference of opinion over these nonessential matters should in no wise be the basis of schism among Christians? First and foremost, we should agree on all points. But since all men are

somewhat beclouded with ignorance, either we must leave no church remaining, or we must condone delusion in those matters which can go unknown without harm to the sum of religion and without loss of salvation. But here I would not support even the slightest errors with the thought of fostering them through flattery and connivance. But I say we must not thoughtlessly forsake the church because of any petty dissensions" (Calvin, *Institutes*, 4.1.12).

39 In defending the doctrine of justification by faith alone as the church's uniting doctrine, Martin Luther rightly said, "This doctrine [justification] is the head and cornerstone. It alone begets, nourishes, builds, preserves, and defends the church of God; and without it the church of God cannot exist for one hour." And "When the article of justification has fallen, everything has fallen." Martin Luther, *Luther's Works*, vols. 30.2 and 40.1, ed. Jaroslav Pelikan and Helmut T. Lehmann (Philadelphia, PA: Muehlenberg and Fortress, and St. Louis, MO: Concordia, 1955–86), 651 and 72.

40 Thomas Watson, *A Puritan Golden Treasury*, comp. I. D. E. Thomas (Carlisle, PA: Banner of Truth, 2000), 304.